EMMANUEL JOSEPH

Pulse Check, Aligning Productivity, Mindfulness, and Relationships for a Fuller Life

Copyright © 2025 by Emmanuel Joseph

All rights reserved. No part of this publication may be reproduced, stored or transmitted in any form or by any means, electronic, mechanical, photocopying, recording, scanning, or otherwise without written permission from the publisher. It is illegal to copy this book, post it to a website, or distribute it by any other means without permission.

First edition

*This book was professionally typeset on Reedsy.
Find out more at reedsy.com*

Contents

1	Chapter 1: The Quest for Balance	1
2	Chapter 2: Defining Productivity	3
3	Chapter 3: The Art of Mindfulness	4
4	Chapter 4: Building Strong Relationships	5
5	Chapter 5: Aligning Productivity and Mindfulness	6
6	Chapter 6: Cultivating Mindful Relationships	7
7	Chapter 7: The Role of Self-Care in Productivity	8
8	Chapter 8: Embracing Imperfection	9
9	Chapter 9: The Power of Gratitude	10
10	Chapter 10: Finding Purpose in Productivity	11
11	Chapter 11: Mindfulness in the Workplace	12
12	Chapter 12: The Impact of Technology on Relationships	13
13	Chapter 13: Balancing Professional and Personal Life	14
14	Chapter 14: Nurturing Mindfulness in Children	15
15	Chapter 15: The Synergy of Mindfulness and Productivity	16
16	Chapter 16: Creating a Mindful Community	17
17	Chapter 17: Living a Fuller Life	18

1

Chapter 1: The Quest for Balance

In our fast-paced world, achieving balance can feel like a pipe dream. Many of us juggle work, family, and personal pursuits, often feeling overwhelmed. The key to balance lies in the heart of three fundamental pillars: productivity, mindfulness, and relationships. When these elements align, we can lead a more fulfilling life. This chapter introduces the core concepts and sets the stage for our journey towards equilibrium.

Imagine starting your day with a clear mind and a focused heart. The noise of distractions fades, and you find yourself navigating tasks effortlessly. This level of productivity isn't a myth; it's the result of conscious effort and strategic planning. In this chapter, we'll explore how to harness productivity techniques without compromising our mental and emotional well-being.

Mindfulness, often considered the antidote to modern chaos, plays a crucial role in maintaining balance. It's about being present, fully engaged in the moment, and aware of our thoughts and feelings. By cultivating mindfulness, we can reduce stress, improve focus, and enhance our overall quality of life. This chapter delves into practical mindfulness practices that can be seamlessly integrated into daily routines.

Relationships are the bedrock of a fulfilled life. Strong connections with family, friends, and colleagues provide emotional support, boost happiness, and foster a sense of belonging. However, nurturing these relationships requires time, effort, and genuine communication. This chapter offers insights into building and maintaining healthy, meaningful relationships while balancing productivity and mindfulness.

2

Chapter 2: Defining Productivity

Productivity is more than just getting things done; it's about achieving meaningful outcomes efficiently. In this chapter, we explore the true essence of productivity and dispel common myths. Productivity is not about working harder or longer but working smarter. It's about prioritizing tasks, setting realistic goals, and managing time effectively.

Time management techniques, such as the Pomodoro Technique, help in breaking work into manageable chunks, preventing burnout. Tools like to-do lists and digital planners keep us organized and on track. This chapter provides practical tips and tricks for enhancing productivity without sacrificing mental well-being. Emphasizing the importance of breaks and self-care is crucial to maintaining high productivity levels.

Moreover, productivity is deeply personal. What works for one person may not work for another. Understanding our unique work styles and preferences enables us to create personalized productivity systems. This chapter encourages self-reflection and experimentation to discover what truly maximizes our efficiency and satisfaction.

It's essential to recognize that productivity extends beyond professional life. Personal projects, hobbies, and self-care activities are equally important. Balancing work and personal life ensures we remain motivated and avoid burnout. This chapter highlights the significance of holistic productivity, encompassing all aspects of life.

3

Chapter 3: The Art of Mindfulness

Mindfulness, rooted in ancient traditions, has gained modern relevance as a powerful tool for mental and emotional well-being. In this chapter, we explore the origins of mindfulness and its contemporary applications. Mindfulness is about paying attention to the present moment without judgment. It's about observing our thoughts and emotions with curiosity and compassion.

Practicing mindfulness can be as simple as taking a few deep breaths or savoring a cup of tea. Mindful meditation, even for a few minutes a day, can significantly reduce stress and enhance focus. This chapter offers various mindfulness exercises and techniques that can be easily incorporated into daily routines, regardless of busy schedules.

The benefits of mindfulness extend beyond individual well-being. Mindful communication enhances relationships by fostering empathy and understanding. By being present in conversations, we build deeper connections and resolve conflicts more effectively. This chapter provides strategies for practicing mindfulness in interactions with others.

Mindfulness also plays a crucial role in productivity. By staying present and focused, we can tackle tasks more efficiently and creatively. This chapter explores the synergy between mindfulness and productivity, highlighting how mindfulness practices can boost our work performance and overall sense of fulfillment.

4

Chapter 4: Building Strong Relationships

Relationships are the cornerstone of a fulfilling life. In this chapter, we delve into the importance of building and nurturing strong connections with family, friends, and colleagues. Healthy relationships provide emotional support, enhance well-being, and contribute to our overall happiness.

Effective communication is the foundation of strong relationships. This chapter explores various communication styles and techniques, emphasizing the importance of active listening and empathy. By understanding and validating others' perspectives, we build trust and deepen our connections.

Quality time and shared experiences are vital for relationship building. In our busy lives, it's essential to prioritize moments of genuine connection. This chapter offers practical suggestions for creating meaningful interactions, whether through regular family dinners, heartfelt conversations, or engaging in activities together.

Conflict resolution is another critical aspect of maintaining healthy relationships. Disagreements are inevitable, but how we handle them determines the strength of our bonds. This chapter provides strategies for resolving conflicts constructively, fostering mutual respect and understanding.

5

Chapter 5: Aligning Productivity and Mindfulness

P roductivity and mindfulness may seem like opposing forces, but they can harmoniously coexist. In this chapter, we explore the intersection of these two concepts and how aligning them can lead to a more balanced life. Mindful productivity is about being intentional and present in our work, enhancing focus and efficiency.

Mindful productivity practices, such as setting clear intentions and taking mindful breaks, can transform our work habits. This chapter provides practical tips for integrating mindfulness into productivity routines, helping us stay grounded and focused.

Moreover, aligning productivity with mindfulness reduces stress and prevents burnout. By being mindful of our limits and prioritizing self-care, we create sustainable work habits. This chapter emphasizes the importance of balance and self-compassion in achieving long-term productivity.

Ultimately, aligning productivity and mindfulness enhances our overall well-being. By being present and intentional in our actions, we experience greater satisfaction and fulfillment. This chapter encourages readers to experiment with mindful productivity practices and discover what works best for them.

6

Chapter 6: Cultivating Mindful Relationships

Mindfulness can transform our relationships by fostering deeper connections and understanding. In this chapter, we explore how to cultivate mindful relationships and enhance our interactions with others. Mindful relationships are built on empathy, active listening, and genuine presence.

Being present in conversations is a key aspect of mindful relationships. This chapter provides techniques for practicing active listening and staying fully engaged in interactions. By showing genuine interest and understanding, we build trust and strengthen our bonds.

Mindful communication also involves being aware of our own emotions and reactions. This chapter offers strategies for managing emotions and responding calmly in challenging situations. By practicing emotional regulation, we create a positive and supportive environment for our relationships.

Moreover, mindfulness encourages us to appreciate and cherish our loved ones. This chapter highlights the importance of gratitude and positive affirmations in nurturing relationships. By expressing appreciation and acknowledging the value of our connections, we deepen our emotional bonds.

7

Chapter 7: The Role of Self-Care in Productivity

Self-care is often overlooked in the pursuit of productivity, but it's essential for long-term success and well-being. In this chapter, we explore the role of self-care in productivity and how it contributes to a balanced life. Self-care involves taking deliberate actions to nurture our physical, mental, and emotional health.

Prioritizing self-care enhances our ability to stay focused and motivated. This chapter provides practical self-care strategies, such as regular exercise, adequate sleep, and healthy nutrition. By taking care of our bodies, we boost our energy levels and overall productivity.

Mental self-care is equally important. This chapter offers techniques for managing stress, such as mindfulness meditation and relaxation exercises. By taking breaks and practicing self-compassion, we prevent burnout and maintain high levels of productivity.

Emotional self-care involves nurturing our relationships and seeking support when needed. This chapter emphasizes the importance of building a strong support network and seeking help during challenging times. By prioritizing self-care, we create a foundation for sustainable productivity and well-being.

8

Chapter 8: Embracing Imperfection

Perfectionism can be a major barrier to productivity and well-being. In this chapter, we explore the concept of embracing imperfection and how it can enhance our lives. Perfectionism often leads to unrealistic expectations and self-criticism, hindering our progress and happiness.

Embracing imperfection involves accepting ourselves and our work as they are. This chapter provides strategies for overcoming perfectionism, such as setting realistic goals and practicing self-compassion. By letting go of the need for perfection, we free ourselves to take risks and grow.

Moreover, embracing imperfection encourages creativity and innovation. This chapter highlights the value of experimentation and learning from mistakes. By viewing failures as opportunities for growth, we develop resilience and adaptability.

Ultimately, embracing imperfection fosters a positive and growth-oriented mindset. This chapter encourages readers to celebrate their achievements, no matter how small, and to appreciate the journey of self-improvement.

9

Chapter 9: The Power of Gratitude

Gratitude is a powerful practice that can transform our mindset and enhance our well-being. In this chapter, we explore the benefits of gratitude and how to incorporate it into our daily lives. Gratitude involves recognizing and appreciating the positive aspects of our lives, fostering a sense of contentment and happiness.

Practicing gratitude can be as simple as keeping a gratitude journal or expressing thanks to others. This chapter provides practical tips for cultivating a gratitude practice, such as setting aside time each day to reflect on what we're thankful for. By focusing on the positives, we shift our perspective and boost our overall well-being.

Gratitude also enhances our relationships by fostering a sense of connection and appreciation. This chapter explores how expressing gratitude to others strengthens our bonds and creates a positive environment. By acknowledging the contributions and kindness of others, we build deeper and more meaningful relationships.

Moreover, gratitude promotes resilience and optimism. This chapter highlights the role of gratitude in overcoming challenges and maintaining a positive outlook. By cultivating a grateful mindset, we navigate life's ups and downs with greater ease and grace.

10

Chapter 10: Finding Purpose in Productivity

Purpose-driven productivity is about aligning our actions with our core values and goals. In this chapter, we explore how to find and integrate purpose into our daily tasks. Purpose gives our work meaning, motivates us to persevere through challenges, and enhances our sense of fulfillment.

Identifying our purpose involves self-reflection and introspection. This chapter provides exercises to help readers discover their values, passions, and long-term goals. By understanding what truly matters to us, we can align our tasks and priorities with our purpose.

Purpose-driven productivity also involves setting meaningful goals. This chapter offers strategies for goal-setting, such as the SMART framework (Specific, Measurable, Achievable, Relevant, Time-bound). By setting clear and achievable goals, we stay focused and motivated.

Moreover, purpose-driven productivity fosters a sense of satisfaction and accomplishment. This chapter encourages readers to celebrate their progress and achievements, no matter how small. By acknowledging our efforts, we reinforce our motivation and commitment to our purpose.

11

Chapter 11: Mindfulness in the Workplace

The workplace can be a source of stress, but incorporating mindfulness can transform our work experience. In this chapter, we explore how to practice mindfulness in professional settings. Mindfulness at work involves being present, focused, and aware of our thoughts and emotions.

Mindful work practices, such as taking mindful breaks and practicing deep breathing, can reduce stress and enhance productivity. This chapter provides practical tips for integrating mindfulness into the workday, helping us stay calm and focused.

Mindfulness also improves workplace relationships. By practicing mindful communication, we foster empathy and understanding with colleagues. This chapter offers strategies for building positive and supportive work relationships through mindfulness.

Moreover, mindfulness enhances creativity and problem-solving skills. By staying present and open-minded, we approach challenges with a fresh perspective. This chapter explores how mindfulness can boost innovation and efficiency in the workplace.

12

Chapter 12: The Impact of Technology on Relationships

Technology has revolutionized how we connect with others, but it also poses challenges to our relationships. In this chapter, we explore the impact of technology on our connections and how to navigate the digital landscape mindfully. Technology offers convenience and accessibility, but it can also lead to distractions and superficial interactions.

Mindful technology use involves setting boundaries and being intentional about our digital interactions. This chapter provides tips for managing screen time, reducing distractions, and prioritizing face-to-face connections. By using technology mindfully, we can enhance our relationships and well-being.

Moreover, technology offers opportunities for maintaining long-distance relationships and connecting with new people. This chapter explores how to leverage technology for meaningful connections while avoiding its pitfalls. By balancing digital and in-person interactions, we create a harmonious relationship with technology.

Ultimately, mindful technology use fosters deeper and more authentic connections. This chapter encourages readers to reflect on their digital habits and make conscious choices that enhance their relationships and overall quality of life.

13

Chapter 13: Balancing Professional and Personal Life

Achieving a balance between professional and personal life is essential for overall well-being. In this chapter, we explore strategies for maintaining equilibrium between work and personal pursuits. Balancing professional and personal life involves setting boundaries, prioritizing tasks, and managing time effectively.

Work-life balance is not a one-size-fits-all concept; it varies for each individual. This chapter encourages readers to reflect on their unique needs and preferences and create personalized balance strategies. By understanding our priorities, we can allocate time and energy to what truly matters.

Moreover, work-life balance involves making intentional choices and setting realistic expectations. This chapter offers practical tips for managing work demands, such as delegating tasks and saying no when necessary. By being mindful of our limits, we prevent burnout and maintain a healthy balance.

Ultimately, achieving work-life balance enhances our overall quality of life. This chapter emphasizes the importance of self-care, relaxation, and spending quality time with loved ones. By prioritizing balance, we create a fulfilling and sustainable lifestyle.

14

Chapter 14: Nurturing Mindfulness in Children

Teaching mindfulness to children can have a profound impact on their development and well-being. In this chapter, we explore how to nurture mindfulness in children and create a mindful family environment. Mindfulness helps children develop emotional regulation, focus, and resilience.

Mindful parenting involves modeling mindfulness practices and creating a calm and supportive environment. This chapter provides tips for incorporating mindfulness into family routines, such as mindful breathing exercises and gratitude practices. By practicing mindfulness together, families strengthen their bonds and overall well-being.

Moreover, mindfulness helps children navigate challenges and build positive relationships. This chapter offers strategies for teaching children mindfulness techniques, such as body scans and mindful listening. By equipping children with mindfulness skills, we empower them to thrive emotionally and socially.

Ultimately, nurturing mindfulness in children lays the foundation for a fulfilling and balanced life. This chapter encourages parents and caregivers to embrace mindfulness as a family practice and create a supportive environment for children's growth and development.

15

Chapter 15: The Synergy of Mindfulness and Productivity

Mindfulness and productivity are not mutually exclusive; they complement each other in powerful ways. In this chapter, we explore the synergy between mindfulness and productivity and how to harness their combined benefits. Mindful productivity involves being present and intentional in our actions, enhancing focus and efficiency.

Integrating mindfulness into productivity practices, such as setting clear intentions and taking mindful breaks, can transform our work habits. This chapter provides practical tips for aligning mindfulness with productivity routines, helping us stay grounded and focused.

Moreover, mindful productivity reduces stress and prevents burnout. By being mindful of our limits and prioritizing self-care, we create sustainable work habits. This chapter emphasizes the importance of balance and self-compassion in achieving long-term productivity.

Ultimately, the synergy of mindfulness and productivity enhances our overall well-being. By being present and intentional in our actions, we experience greater satisfaction and fulfillment. This chapter encourages readers to experiment with mindful productivity practices and discover what works best for them.

16

Chapter 16: Creating a Mindful Community

Building a mindful community involves fostering connections and support among like-minded individuals. In this chapter, we explore how to create and nurture a mindful community, enhancing our sense of belonging and well-being. A mindful community provides emotional support, encourages personal growth, and promotes collective well-being.

Creating a mindful community involves practicing mindfulness together and sharing experiences. This chapter offers tips for organizing mindful gatherings, such as meditation groups, mindfulness workshops, and community service projects. By coming together with shared intentions, we create a positive and supportive environment.

Moreover, a mindful community fosters a sense of accountability and motivation. This chapter explores how community members can support each other in their mindfulness and productivity journeys. By sharing goals and progress, we inspire and encourage one another.

Ultimately, a mindful community enhances our overall quality of life. This chapter emphasizes the importance of connection, collaboration, and mutual support. By building a mindful community, we create a network of individuals committed to personal and collective well-being.

17

Chapter 17: Living a Fuller Life

Living a fuller life involves aligning productivity, mindfulness, and relationships to create a balanced and fulfilling existence. In this final chapter, we reflect on the journey we've taken and the insights we've gained. A fuller life is not about perfection but about continuous growth and intentional living.

Living a fuller life involves embracing our unique paths and making conscious choices that align with our values and goals. This chapter encourages readers to continue their mindfulness and productivity practices, nurturing their relationships and personal growth.

Moreover, living a fuller life involves celebrating our achievements and embracing the present moment. This chapter highlights the importance of gratitude, self-compassion, and joy in our daily lives. By appreciating the journey and our progress, we create a sense of fulfillment and contentment.

Ultimately, living a fuller life is a lifelong journey of growth, connection, and mindfulness. This chapter encourages readers to embrace their unique journeys and continue striving for balance and fulfillment. By aligning productivity, mindfulness, and relationships, we create a richer, more meaningful life.

Pulse Check: Aligning Productivity, Mindfulness, and Relationships for a Fuller Life

Book Description:

CHAPTER 17: LIVING A FULLER LIFE

In the hustle and bustle of modern life, finding balance can feel like a daunting task. "Pulse Check" offers a refreshing perspective on achieving harmony by aligning three essential pillars: productivity, mindfulness, and relationships. This insightful guide takes you on a journey to a fuller life, where efficiency meets presence, and connections thrive.

Through 17 thought-provoking chapters, the book delves into the core of what it means to be productive without sacrificing your mental and emotional well-being. It introduces practical techniques to harness productivity, integrate mindfulness into daily routines, and build strong, meaningful relationships.

"Pulse Check" emphasizes the importance of self-care, gratitude, and embracing imperfection. It explores the synergy between mindfulness and productivity, offering actionable tips to create sustainable habits. The book also highlights the role of technology in our connections and provides strategies for mindful digital interactions.

Whether you're seeking to enhance your professional life, nurture personal relationships, or find inner peace, "Pulse Check" is your comprehensive guide to living a balanced and fulfilling life. Embark on this transformative journey and discover how aligning productivity, mindfulness, and relationships can lead to a richer, more meaningful existence.

www.ingramcontent.com/pod-product-compliance
Lightning Source LLC
LaVergne TN
LVHW010446070526
838199LV00066B/6222